Salem and Marblehead

Salem and Marblehead

by Peter E. Randall

Down East Books
Camden, Maine

To my grandmother, Frances Randall

Copyright © 1983 by Peter E. Randall
Library of Congress Catalog Card no. 83-70547
ISBN 0-89272-163-4
Design by Peter E. Randall
Composition by Roxmont Graphics
Manufactured in the United States of America

10   9   8   7   6   5   4   3   2   1

Down East Books / *Camden, Maine*

Other Down East Books by Peter E. Randall:
All Creation and the Isles of Shoals
New Hampshire — Four Seasons
Newburyport and the Merrimack
Portsmouth and the Piscataqua
115 Country Inns of New Hampshire and Vermont

*(page one) The Cook-Oliver House, 142 Federal Street, was
designed by Samuel McIntire in 1802–03 and has one of his finest
fences. The house was built for Captain Samuel Cook and later
owned by his son-in-law Henry K. Oliver, a mayor of Salem
and, later, Lawrence.*

*(preceding page) Salem Common is surrounded by many Federal
period mansions. This view is toward Washington Square North.
The bandstand, crowned with a pineapple finial, was erected in
1926 to replace a nineteenth-century structure.*

*(front cover) Number 12 Chestnut Street, left, built for town
treasurer Jonathan Hodges in 1805, and number 10 Chestnut
Street, built for merchant Nathaniel Robinson in 1808, are
typical of the Federal period mansions along this architecturally
important street.*

*(rear cover) Carved eagle tops the Custom House at the Salem
Maritime National Historic Site.*

*The Goult-Pickman House, adjacent to the Charter Street Cemetery,
was built prior to 1660. Private.*

Preface

Mt. Washington, the state of New Hampshire, the Isles of Shoals, Portsmouth and Newburyport, each the subject of a previous book, are places with which I am familiar. Salem and Marblehead were new communities for me, and I had to learn my way around each town in order to discover their treasures and to become familiar enough to describe what I found.

The difficulties of such a task were made much easier with the support of many people, and in particular: Bryant F. Tolles, Jr., and Ann Farnam of the Essex Institute; Ed Stevenson and gardener extraordinaire Dan Foley of the House of Seven Gables; Helen Usher, Mrs. Stephen Phillips, Dorothy Freeman, Mrs. John Pickering, Donald Costin, and John Frayler.

In Marblehead I received indispensible assistance from Betty Hunt of the Marblehead Historical Society and from her brother Herbert Haskell, who accompanied me on the climb to the top of Abbot Hall. In all cases, errors of fact remain my own.

As a professional tourist, I am happy to offer my own view of Salem and Marblehead to add to the appreciation of residents and visitors alike. It was not my intention to prepare an all-purpose guidebook to either community but to offer a glimpse of these two ancient towns. Many places simply could not be included, but part of the enjoyment of both Salem and Marblehead is to wander at one's own pace to discover the treasures that each town offers.

Contents

A Guide for the Visitor

*Pickering Wharf with buildings of the Salem
Maritime National Historic Site in the background.*

Salem

For many people, "doing Salem" means a drive down Chestnut Street and a stop at the House of the Seven Gables, perhaps the most visited single historic house in New England. But Salem has much more to offer: more than twenty houses and historic buildings open to the public, two major museums, a variety of street fairs and musical events, and many antiques and contemporary goods shops at Pickering Wharf, East India Square, Essex Street Mall, Salem Marketplace, and throughout the city.

In the following pages we offer a glimpse of a number of Salem's attractions, especially those associated with its history. Generally, everything is open daily from late May through mid-October. Some houses are not open every day of the week but one cannot see everything in a single day anyway.

We have listed the general open periods for each place, but the Salem Chamber of Commerce (Old Town Hall, 32 Derby Square, tel. 617-744-0004) annually publishes a free brochure listing all attractions and their exact opening and closing dates, hours, and fees. The free *Best of Salem* booklet (Box 4445, Salem, MA 01970) is a handy guide to accommodations, dining, shopping, and historic attractions.

Salem is located about forty-five minutes' drive north of Boston. Commuter trains from North Station and buses from Haymarket Square provide regular service to Salem from Boston. When driving to Salem follow Route 114 from either Route 128 (traveling north) or from I-95 (traveling south). The parking situation is most difficult in the vicinity of Pickering Wharf. There is a parking lot on Congress Street and parking at Riley Plaza, the East India Square Parking Garage, or adjacent to the Peabody Museum. From these locations one can walk to Essex Institute, Peabody Museum, or Pickering Wharf area. (See map, inside front cover.) There is ample curbside parking along Chestnut Street, and one could spend a quiet afternoon just walking along Federal, Flint, Essex, Chestnut, and Broad streets. Here it is easy to imagine what this area was like over a hundred years ago because changes have been minimal. Some of the "new" buildings are a hundred years old.

Because of the many one-way streets in the Chestnut Street Historic District, we recommend the following route, which is also the best way to visit the historic houses in this area: When entering Salem from Route 114, turn right on Federal Street. At the corner is the Peirce-Nichols house. Further down on Federal is the Assembly House. Just beyond the Assembly House turn left on Flint Street, then turn left onto Essex Street. At the end of Essex, adjacent to the intersection with North Street, are located Greymoor, the Ropes Mansion, First Church, and the Witch House. From Essex Street, turn right onto Summer Street, go past the intersection with Chestnut, then turn right onto Broad Street to find the Pickering House. Follow Broad Street to Flint and turn right, travel two blocks and turn right again onto Chestnut Street. The Stephen Phillips House is on the left, and near the end of the street is Hamilton Hall.

At the end of Chestnut Street, go straight ahead on Norman, circle around Riley Plaza (large parking area) and follow New Derby Street to Pickering Wharf, the Salem Maritime National Historic Site, and the House of the Seven Gables (large parking lot).

After leaving the House of the Seven Gables, turn left on Carlton Street, follow to Essex Street, then turn left on Essex and follow to the stop light. Directly across Hawthorne Boulevard are the buildings of the Essex Institute, and beyond on the left side is the Peabody Museum. Signs indicate parking lots. From either parking lot one can easily walk to Salem Common and the Witch Museum.

Salem has a number of fine restaurants and less formal places to have lunch. Ample overnight accommodations are available both in Salem and in surrounding communities.

Salem hosts nearly one million visitors each year, and a large portion of these travelers come in the prime months of July and August. This area of New England is also delightful in May, June, and September when there are fewer people around, especially at the more popular attractions. In all cases, group tours are welcome only with advance reservations.

Marblehead

For the visitor, the most interesting part of Marblehead is the old town, especially the section between Washington Street and the waterfront. On or near Washington Street are Abbot Hall, the Lee Mansion, the King Hooper Mansion, St. Michael's Church and the Old North Church, the only historic buildings in Marblehead regularly open to the public. Although

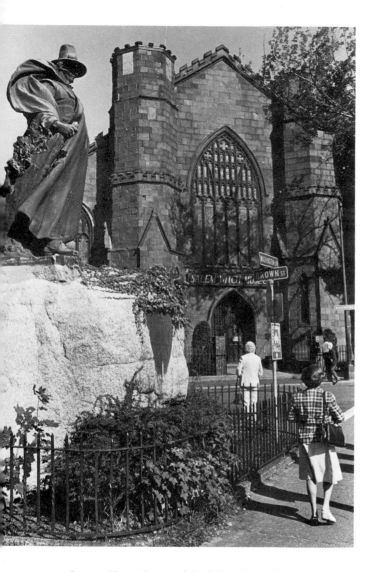

Statue of Roger Conant, Salem's founder, and the Salem Witch Museum at the corner of Brown Street and Washington Square North. The museum, one of the city's most popular attractions, has dioramas, with sound and light, depicting the witchcraft hysteria of 1692.

most of the old town is a historic district, virtually all of the buildings are private homes, and the privacy of residents should be respected.

Since Marblehead has few overnight accommodations, most visitors are day-trippers. They soon realize that the town is best seen on foot or from a bicycle. The streets — narrow, winding, and lined with picturesque eighteenth- and nineteenth-century homes — are not conducive to traffic or parking. As the map on the inside rear cover shows, the old town is a small area, so it is wise to find a parking place and then walk or bicycle.

One of the joys of Marblehead is the opportunity to explore and discover on your own. Unlike Salem, which offers enough house tours to keep one busy for a couple of days, Marblehead encourages visitors to see just a couple of house interiors, then spend the rest of their time poking about at one of three waterfront parks, in the Old Burying Ground, along one of many winding streets, or in any of several antiques and specialty shops.

For those who want to be more organized in their travels, the booklet *The Lure of Marblehead* offers eight walking tours and much data about particular houses in the town.

At the foot of State Street is the town landing, with clean rest rooms and a small parking lot. The attendant is helpful with directions. Several waterfront restaurants and a number of lunchrooms offer a variety of meals but one can also bring a lunch to the park and enjoy the activity in the harbor.

The Marblehead Chamber of Commerce, 62 Pleasant Street, Box 76, Marblehead, MA 01945 (tel. 617-631-2868) publishes an annual booklet with a variety of information for visitors.

For people using mass transportation, Marblehead is served several times daily by bus (via Lynn) from Boston's Haymarket Square. And since Marblehead is called the Yachting Capital of America, there are ample services for the seagoing visitor.

A Brief History of Salem

With more than 350 years of recorded history, Salem ranks as one of the oldest communities in America. Roger Conant, after unsuccessfully trying to settle on Cape Ann in 1623, arrived in Salem (then called Naumkeag) with a small group in 1626. Conant had a patent to settle the north shore of Massachusetts but civil and religious turmoil in England caused many other people to seek sanctuary in the New World as well. In 1628 John Endicott and his followers came to Salem with another patent allowing them to share the area with Conant's settlers. A third group, led by John Winthrop, arrived in 1630 on board the ship *Arbella*. Winthrop's charter surpassed the previous two, and he was appointed governor. He soon moved the capital of the colony from Salem to Cambridge.

Those early Salem settlers, who named their town as a variant of the Jewish word for peace — *Shalom* - were seekers of religious freedom. The group included many educated men, and they acted swiftly to establish a church and pursue their own form of religion. Civil and religious authority were combined by these stern people, who insisted on strict enforcement of their rules. Those rules generated constant conflict with the rough-and-ready fishermen of neighboring Marblehead. Established by the English as a fishing station in 1629 and originally called Marble Harbor, Marblehead was settled by people more concerned with making a living than with religious freedom. Although legally part of Salem, Marblehead was not Puritan and the people had no control over the laws imposed upon them, so for the most part the fishermen ignored those laws. Drunkenness, adultery, and ignoring the Sabbath were the charges leveled against Marblehead by the Salem residents. The Puritans had little success in enforcing their rules, and in 1648, Salem voted to allow Marblehead to become a separate town.

The witchcraft trials of 1692 may shock us today, but it should be remembered that there was at that time a widespread belief in witches as an explanation for the unknown. Similar trials and executions occurred elsewhere in Europe and New England. The Salem events are especially grisly because of the number of people involved in such a short period of time. The tragedy of 1692 began when a group of teenage girls from the part of Salem that is now Danvers learned black magic and tricks from the West Indian woman Tituba.

After the girls began to tease and harass people in the community, they were examined by a doctor who proclaimed them bewitched because the girls didn't admit their trickery. When the community leaders sought to learn the identities of the witches, the girls blamed three women in the community. More accusations followed, and within nine months, twenty people were executed and more than 150 others were jailed.

The terrifying events came to an end when the wives of prominent community leaders were accused. People began to reconsider their ugly acts. Eventually everybody in jail was freed and the government even provided some payment to the families of the executed.

Salem's fine harbor and the proximity of excellent fishing grounds turned the community's economy toward the sea. By the early 1700s, Salem's captains were part of the brisk trade between the colonies, Europe, and the West Indies. New England's fine codfish was shipped to Spain. The poorer fish, lumber, and other raw goods found ready markets in the Caribbean. Such West India goods as molasses and sugar were either brought back to Salem or transported directly to England. This trade occupied the seaport until the outbreak of the Revolution.

When the war with England began America had no navy, but merchants soon armed their ships and began to ravage the British fleets as privateers. Over 158 Salem ships, manned by thousands of sailors, captured 445 such prizes, aiding the war effort — and incidentally enriching the merchants, captains, and crews.

When the war ended, Salem's many ships, no longer limited to ports approved by the English, sailed to the far corners of the Earth seeking profitable cargoes. Salem's golden age began. Her ships opened American trade with Russia, the Cape of Good Hope, India, Java, Japan, and China. A Salem captain discovered wild pepper growing in Sumatra, and for twenty years Salem controlled this lucrative market. By 1801, Salem had forty-five wharfs. Between the end of the Revolution and the War of 1812, Salem boomed as money flowed into the coffers of merchants and shipowners. Most of Salem's architectural treasures and fine furnishings date from these years.

Of the many important people who lived during this period, three men stand out: Derby, Bowditch, and McIntire. Elias Hasket Derby (1739 – 1799), son of a wealthy merchant, married Elizabeth Crowninshield, daughter of an equally rich family. Their first home is now part of the Salem Maritime National Historic Site. Derby expanded his father's holdings and became America's first millionaire. During the Revolution, he outfitted one hundred privateers, and after the war his ships pioneered trade throughout the world. Although the China trade was lucrative, that market was soon overwhelmed with American goods, so Derby's ships went to India and the East Indies.

When Derby sent his first ship to Manila in 1796, the supercargo was young Nathaniel Bowditch of Salem. Bowditch in later years combined his interests in science and in the sea to compile *The New American Practical Navigator*, a nautical guide, updated and still in use today. Derby and the other shipowners had the wealth to outfit ships for foreign ports; Bowditch supplied the knowledge that assisted the ship captains in reaching those ports and returning home. Bowditch's birthplace is located on Kimball Court, behind the Witch Museum. For most of his life he lived in a house now owned by the city and located on North Street adjacent to the Witch House.

Statue of Nathanial Hawthorne on Hawthorne Boulevard.

The wealth that poured into Salem was not left idle. Merchants and shipowners built larger vessels and bankrolled them on more exotic voyages, usually resulting in even more riches. The affluent had more than enough money to satisfy their own personal comfort as well. Salem had many fine craftsmen, but it was Samuel McIntire (1757 – 1811) who had the skill and the artistic taste to transform the character of the city.

Woodcarver, architect, and carpenter, McIntire worked steadily for Derby and other merchants, designing private homes and public buildings. The Assembly House and Hamilton Hall, the Peirce-Nichols House, and the Pingree-Gardner House all bear his

The Nathaniel Bowditch House, now owned by the city, on North Street.

touch in architecture, woodwork, or furniture. Many of his individual pieces are found in the Essex Institute and elsewhere in collections throughout the country, although he was content to work mostly in his native city. McIntire developed the neoclassical style to a high degree. His basic designs came from English architectural books popular in the period but his particular execution of the designs was much admired throughout New England, and many other builders were inspired by his work.

By the time of McIntire's death in 1811, Salem, along with other New England seaports, was handicapped by the Embargo Acts. Salem captains went privateering again in the War of 1812. As late as 1825 there were nearly two hundred vessels operating out of Salem. Her ships continued to seek out new ports in the Pacific and along the coast of Africa but eventually Salem's harbor proved to be too shallow for the newer, larger ships such as the clippers. By the 1850s railroads provided easy transportation from the back country to larger ports such as Boston. Activity at the smaller ports declined, and by the time of the Civil War Salem's prominence as a seaport was over.

There is, of course, one other individual whose name will ever be associated with Salem, and that is Nathaniel Hawthorne (1804–1864). A native of Salem, he was a descendant of witch-trial judge John Hathorne. While a student at Bowdoin College Nathaniel added the "w" to his name, perhaps to separate himself from the infamous judge. He lived in Salem at various times, and it was during the time that he worked as surveyor of the port in the Custom House from 1846 to 1849 that he apparently gathered much of the background material used in *The Scarlet Letter* and *The House of the Seven Gables*. A cousin lived in "the Gables" and Hawthorne learned many stories from her. Although he did not live in Salem on a regular basis, he often returned to his native city for lengthy periods. As his novels became famous, people began to seek him out in Salem. People are still fascinated with Hawthorne, and their enthusiasm has made the Gables the leading attraction in the city. Most of the other houses with which he was associated still exist although they are not open to the public. Visitors driving along Hawthorne Boulevard can view his statue, located in the small park at the junction with Essex Street.

After the Civil War, Salem, along with most of New England, developed manufacturing businesses, particularly textile mills. Much of the architecture developed during the periods of earliest settlement through the early 1800s remained, but the prosperity resulting from manufacturing fostered continued building. Today Salem has as many Victorian buildings as it does earlier ones, but the public fancy runs to Georgian and Federal period architecture.

Salem people recognized the importance of their architectural treasures by the turn of the century, and both individuals and institutions began to preserve many of the buildings that are today open to the public.

The belief in preservation continues, and was most recently expressed in the mid-1970s when the commercial architecture of Salem's downtown was rehabilitated as part of the Essex Street Mall.

11

Behind the institute's Essex Street buildings are the Crowninshield Gardens complete with Beebe Summer House (ca. 1800).

Essex Institute
132 Essex Street

One of America's oldest and most respected regional historical societies, the Essex Institute began in 1848 with the merger of the Essex Historical Society (incorporated 1821) and the Essex County Natural History Society (1836). The institute was one of the earliest private institutions to become interested in historic preservation when it moved a Quaker meetinghouse to the institute grounds in 1865. The acquisition and extensive restoration of the John Ward House was undertaken in 1910. Today the institue owns six historic furnished houses and manages a seventh, all open to the public. These dwellings are representative of Salem residences from the period of early settlement through the mid-Victorian era. The following pages offer a glimpse of each house.

Equally important for the scholar is the institute's James Duncan Phillips research library. The diverse collection of books, pamphlets, periodicals, manuscripts, letters, photographs, and other material has made this library a major regional research center. Located in the John Tucker Daland House (1851), the library has extensive collections in genealogy and architecture as well as original documents relating to Salem's infamous witch trials of 1692.

Adjacent to the library is Plummer Hall (1857), which houses the portrait gallery and extensive museum collections. For generations the institute has been the repository of historical artifacts that reflect the social changes in the Essex County area since the period of the first settlement. Collections of fine and decorative arts, including painting and sculpture, textiles and costumes, artifacts of everyday life, military items, and tools are on display in the museum and in the furnished houses.

The institute also hosts special exhibits, publishes periodical and special publications, and has an active education program for all grade levels from kindergarten through high school.

The Essex Street complex includes four of the historic houses as well as the Lye-Tapely shoe shop (1830), the Quaker Meetinghouse (1688) with the Vaughan Doll Collection, the Gardner-Pingree Carriage House (1805), the Beebe Summer House (ca. 1800) and the Louise duPont Crowninshield Garden.

The museum and the Pingree-Gardner House are open Tuesday through Saturday and Sunday afternoons throughout the year. The museum is open Mondays June through October. The library and office are open Monday through Friday. The Andrew-Safford House is open one day per week throughout the year, and the other houses are open June through October. Admission is charged for all the buildings, and tickets for each are available at the museum. For further details: The Essex Institute, 132–34 Essex Street, Salem, MA 01970 (tel. 617-744-3390).

The institute's Andrew Oliver Portrait Gallery features paintings, furniture, and other decorative arts.

The Ward House viewed through spring blossoms.

John Ward House
Behind 132 Essex Street

The first of the houses to be restored by Essex Institute, the Ward House was built about 1684. It was moved to its present location and restored between 1910 and 1912. The house passed out of the Ward family in 1816, was used for some forty years as a bakery, then became a tenement. In 1887 the house was willed to the county. Apparently its antiquity was appreciated, because the county commissioners voted to give the house to the institute.

Some twenty-three years elapsed before the offer was accepted and acted upon but the restoration of the house was part of a trend that has since resulted in the preservation of many houses in the city.

As viewed today, the Ward House is a combination of original features and restoration. It was constructed in stages between 1684 and 1732, and its years as bakery and tenement altered both exterior and interior. George Francis Dow, secretary of the institute, coordinated the restoration. He was a pioneer in this field and apparently his plan for the Ward House was to create a typical seventeenth-century dwelling. We know that Dow made extensive notes on his projects but his written material from the Ward House was lost.

The furnishings were selected to represent the typical home of about 1700 and many of the items came from the institute's collection or were purchased by Dow in anticipation of the completed restoration. Among the special collections are the cent shop, weaving room, and the apothecary shop.

Open June through October. Admission charged.

(left) The apothecary shop in the Ward House was furnished with goods purchased from a Salem shop established in 1830. (below) The kitchen.

Andrew-Safford House
13 Washington Square West

Built in 1818–19 for merchant John Andrew and later owned by the Safford family, this house is the residence of the institute's director. Several rooms are open to the public, however.

Constructed in the late neoclassical style, the house is a masterpiece of the period. Among its many unusual features are the tall doric columns on the south side — massive architectural details that served primarily to indicate the owner's great wealth. Andrew had spent seven years as a commission merchant in Russia, and his success in the fur trade allowed him to build what was considered the costliest mansion in New England. The house was occupied by the Safford family from 1871 until it was purchased by the institute in 1947.

(above) The Andrew-Safford House front portico. (left) Victorian parlor with a table and French cabinet made in 1869.

The Empire period parlor set, made in Italy, was a wedding gift to Catherine Peabody Gardner in 1827.

Although the architect/builder of the house is unknown, it does contain elements similar to those found in houses nearby around Washington Square and on Chestnut Street. Many museum houses have required extensive restoration, but this dwelling reflects changes in time from the days of its original construction. With its stable wing, garden, walls, and fences, the house offers a vivid image of early nineteenth-century city life.

Open all year. Admission charged.

(above) The Double
Parlor. (left) Crownin-
shield Memorial Room.

18

Gardner-Pingree House
128 Essex Street

Architect Samuel McIntire designed this house for wealthy merchant John Gardner. Completed in 1805, it is considered to be a McIntire masterpiece. The house unfortunately had to be sold in 1811 when Gardner lost his fortune prior to the outbreak of the War of 1812.

In 1834 David Pingree bought the house. Ninety-nine years later, when his son, David, died, the property was given by the family to the institute. The elder Pingree inherited great wealth and engaged in shipping worldwide. Son David invested his inheritance and became a multimillionaire through management of some seven-hundred thousand acres of family-owned Maine woodlands.

McIntire's design for this house was influenced by the books of English architect Robert Adam. Considered to be one of the finest examples of the Adamesque style, the house inspired similar construction by other wealthy merchants in New England. The severe, monumental facade, topped by a balustrade at the roof, contrasts with the detailed wood and plaster composition ornamentation of the interior. The hall and the double parlor (opposite, above) have many examples of McIntire's favorite details such as the baskets of fruit on the mantlepieces.

The furniture, most of which is from Salem and the North Shore region, was selected to represent the 1815 period. Many pieces are well-documented as to maker and early owners. They are now visual examples of the wealth and sophistication that marked Salem's high society. Handpainted imported nineteenth-century wallpapers accent both the furniture and the architecture of this Federal townhouse.

Open all year. Admission charged.

Exterior of the Gardner-Pingree House is considered one of McIntire's finest.

Crowninshield-Bentley House
126 Essex Street

Crowninshield-Bentley House.

Built at 106 Essex Street for Captain John Crowninshield about 1727, this house was moved to its present location and restored in 1960.

The seafaring Crowninshields were a prominent Salem mercantile family. Captain John's daughter Elizabeth married Elias Hasket Derby, soon to become America's first millionaire, and her brother George married Elias's sister Mary, thus joining the wealthy families in a double knot.

The most famous resident of the house, however, was the Reverend William Bentley. Clergyman as well as naturalist, linguist, scientist, and historian, Bentley boarded with the widow Hannah Crowninshield from 1791 until his death in 1819. During these years he kept a diary. At this time when Salem was undergoing its greatest period of growth, Bentley, who was blessed with intense curiosity and a great intellect, carefully recorded all manner of information about Salem, past and present. His conversations with the oldest inhabitants and his commentary on contemporary subjects have provided scholars with details about Salem that might otherwise have been lost. The diaries have been published in four volumes by the Essex Institute.

The house was altered several times, and the changes show how people expanded their dwellings. The original house consisted of the eastern, or right, side, then about 1761 the western section was added, and in 1794 the house was extensively renovated and the rear ell was built.

Furnishings represent the entire eighteenth century and especially the Queen Anne and Chippendale styles. A few of Dr. Bentley's possessions remain, and the upper east chamber where he boarded has been furnished as he might have done.

Open June through October. Admission charged.

The new kitchen.

Dr. Bentley's bedroom.

21

Ropes Mansion
318 Essex Street

Although Salem's most impressive houses date from the Federal period, the earlier architectural styles are important, too. After visiting Salem in 1766, John Adams wrote "The houses are the most elegant and grand that I have seen in any of the maritime towns."

Adams may well have been referring to such Georgian dwellings as the Ropes Mansion. Built after 1727, the Ropes Mansion has been open to the public since 1912. The 2½-story gambrel dwelling was constructed for merchant Samuel Barnard but it was acquired by Judge Nathaniel Ropes II in 1768 and remained in the family until the death of the judge's great-granddaughter Eliza Ropes in 1907.

The house has been altered several times, the most extensive being in 1835, when a new staircase was installed, five rooms were remodeled in the Greek Revival style, fireplaces were altered and woodwork was changed. In 1894 the house was moved back from the street, a 2½-story addition placed at the rear, and the old kitchen remodeled as a formal dining room.

Four generations of the Ropes family lived in the house, and their possessions are the most notable features. The collections of Nanking porcelain and Irish glass are outstanding. Some of the furnishings are said to have belonged to Judge Ropes and his wife.

When the property was taken over by a board of trustees in 1912, the extensive garden and brick wall were installed. Open to the public without charge, the garden is one of the loveliest in the city. Now owned by the trustees of the Ropes Memorial, the property has been managed by the Essex Institute since 1978.

Open June through October. Admission charged.

(above) A portion of the Ropes Mansion garden.
(opposite below) Dining room of the Ropes Mansion.

(left) Peirce-Nichols House exterior with one of Salem's famous fences. (below) East parlor, altered by McIntire in 1801.

Peirce-Nichols House
80 Federal Street

Built in the 1780s by its first owner, Jerathmiel Peirce, this house is considered to be the first major work of architect Samuel McIntire. Late Georgian in style, the house is unusual because several portions of the interior were altered to the Adamesque style by McIntire himself in 1801.

Peirce became a wealthy India trader after the Revolution. He built this house, and it was on the occasion of the marriage of his daughter Sally to George Nichols that McIntire altered the hall and east parlor and chamber. It is the combination of two superb McIntire styles that makes this house so important.

Peirce was forced to sell the house to satisfy creditors after the War of 1812 and it was acquired at auction by a friend, George Stuart Johonnot. Johonnot's widow, Martha, willed the house back to George Nichols, who, after Sally's death in 1835, married her sister Betsey. Great-granddaughters of the builder sold the house to the Essex Institute in 1917.

When the house was auctioned in 1827, the furniture was sold as well. Fortunately, many pieces, perhaps purchased by John Johonnot or family members, have been reacquired and remain in their original positions today. Of note are the settees in the east parlor, probably carved by McIntire for George and Sally's wedding, and the bed in the neoclassical bedroom.

Open June through October. Admission charged.

*Looking into
the second floor
Georgian bedroom.*

25

Assembly House
138 Federal Street

Another of the Salem buildings associated with Samuel McIntire, the Assembly House was built in 1782 as a public hall and for the next fifteen years it was a center of social and political activity. Receptions for Lafayette and Washington were held here as well as various balls, plays, concerts, and other similar events.

The exact original appearance of this building is unknown but it was remodeled to its present style as a private home by McIntire about 1796. The original proprietors of the building sold their shares to a couple of entrepreneurs who had built a commercial block with a new, larger meeting hall, and the new owners wanted to hold public gatherings in their own building.

McIntire's work on this house is important, for it is one of his earliest uses of the Adamesque style and thus can be compared with his later work in that style at the Peirce-Nichols and Gardner-Pingree houses. His most obvious changes to the Assembly House were on the facade, particularly the four pairs of pilasters added to the second story. A major alteration on the inside was the creation of a second floor. McIntire's wood carving and other embellishments remain in various rooms.

The building was given to the institute in 1964 and was opened to the public in 1972. Many pieces of furniture were given by previous owners. The house is particularly rich in mid-nineteenth-century items acquired in China, India, and Zanzibar by Salem's merchant traders.

Open June through October. Admission charged.

(above) Assembly House dining room with twentieth-century Chinese reproduction wallpaper. (right) The second-floor Victorian parlor. (opposite) Except for the mid-nineteenth-century portico, the facade of the Assembly House reflects McIntire's design.

John Pickering House
18 Broad Street

The John Pickering House, built in 1651, is the oldest house in America continuously occupied by one family. During ten generations of Pickering ownership the house has undergone many changes, the most obvious being its current 1840s Gothic facade.

Family members have been active in political affairs since the days of the second John Pickering (1637–94), who was a selectman. The most famous Pickering was Colonel Timothy, quartermaster general of the Revolutionary Army and later Washington's secretary of state, secretary of war, and postmaster. Portraits of Timothy and items owned by him are on display.

The Pickering house boasts many family heirlooms and furniture by known local craftsmen, as well as many documents and letters from Washington and other prominent statesmen.

The house and property are now part of the non-profit Pickering Foundation, created in 1951. The house is open throughout the year on Mondays from 10 a.m. – 3 p.m. and on Sunday afternoons in the summer. Admission charged. (Tel. 617-744-1647).

(above) A portrait of Timothy Pickering hangs in the dining room. The chairs were made by Theophilis Pickering in 1730. (right) The green bedroom is the last in the Pickering House with old floors and Delft tiles around the fireplace.

Greymoor
329 Essex Street

In a city famed for its early architecture, Greymoor is a pleasant surprise. Salem has about as many Victorian buildings as it does Georgian and Federal, but this is the only one of the former open to the public.

Built during 1871–72 for the James Putnam family, this three-story, Second Empire mansion was for forty years the home of Frank Balch, a chemist and inventor of the Roentgen Scoptic Screen (a device that saved time and expense in making x-rays). From 1920 until 1979, the building was the local American Legion

home. Although well-used by the organization, the house was relatively little damaged when acquired by Donald Costin. Marble fireplaces, stained glass, mouldings, balustrades, and the walnut staircase were among the major elements still intact.

Costin, who had restored and lived in several eighteenth- and early nineteenth-century houses, was intrigued with the idea of restoring and furnishing this later period house. He acquired many pieces from the Governor Ames estate in Boston and collected other items from all over New England. Furnishings in the sitting room are from Gustav Herter, who was the dec-

(right) Front hall. (opposite) Greymoor is one of the few houses furnished to the postbellum period open to the public.

orator for many mansions along New York's Fifth Avenue.

For those who are used to seeing the sparsely decorated houses of earlier periods, each heavily furnished room in Greymoor offers a surprise.

Open by appointment or chance. Admission charged. (Tel. 617-745-6646)

(left) The upper hall is furnished as a music room and features a Rosewood organ. (below) Sitting room. Period prints and paintings accent the furniture. (opposite, above) A twenty-foot Cuban mahogany table (1854) highlights the dining room. The serving ware is Tiffany and the dishes are Derby English china. Although the chandeliers had to be replaced, the doors of walnut, oak, and birdseye maple are original. (below) Bedroom with Empire furnishings.

Federal and Essex Streets

Visitors with a little extra time should park their cars, then walk along these parallel streets. Along with Chestnut Street, these neighborhoods form an important Salem historic district. To stroll along the brick sidewalks, viewing the late eighteenth- and early nineteenth-century houses is to experience Salem the way captains and seamen would have seen the city when returning from a voyage. Especially enjoyable is the section of Federal Street stretching from the Peirce-Nichols House west toward the Assembly House.

Essex Street is one of the oldest in the city and was originally the way to the pastures and a brick kiln at the west side of the community. Federal Street was laid out in 1766.

Federal Street was laid out in 1766, and by 1810 it was lined on both sides by fine houses. (above) Three-story Federal house was built prior to 1810. At left, on the corner of Monroe Street is a house built in 1782 for the widow and son of Nathaniel Gould. (opposite, right) One of the newest buildings along Federal Street is this store and home built to fit its lot in the mid-1850s. (opposite, left) Brick sidewalks and shade trees add to the charm of Federal Street.

(*above*) Essex Grace Church parish house was built prior to 1806. The mansion next-door at 387 Essex Street dates from 1858. (*below*) Bott's Court connects Essex and Chestnut Streets.

Hamilton Hall, on Chestnut Street, designed by Samuel McIntire, was built for the Federalists in 1805 and named for their hero Alexander Hamilton. Constructed as a place for assemblies and social gatherings, Hamilton Hall is still used for that purpose.

Chestnut Street

"This street . . . is one of the finest I ever saw. It has noble sidewalks and the buildings on each side give the impression of comfort and elegance." This quote by an early Salem visitor is still true today.

Considered one of the most architecturally significant streets in America, Chestnut Street was laid out in 1796 when Salem was at the height of its importance as a seaport. An elegant home was the surest sign of success and Salem's wealthy merchants, captains, and ship owners were quick to acquire lots on the new street.

Although Samuel McIntire is often credited with the architecture of these houses, he only did a few of them. Other builders and architects were working in Salem at this time, and their skill is evident in the beauty of the brick and wood houses. Many of these homes still retain their carriage sheds and outbuildings.

Although the Lombardy poplars and elms are now gone, the broad way with its brick sidewalks is little changed from the days when the houses were first built. Now protected as part of a historic district, Chestnut Street is most properly enjoyed by strolling along its walks.

Stephen Phillips's bedroom has rare Chinese rugs, and a J.O.J. Frost painting of Marblehead over the mantle.

Stephen Phillips Memorial Trust House
34 Chestnut Street

This historically interesting house is the only one on Chestnut Street open to the public. It was built in Danvers in the late eighteenth century by Samuel McIntire for Captain Nathaniel West and his wife, Elizabeth Derby. In 1820, the house was cut in half and the front four rooms were moved to this location. A new rear portion of the house was built at this time.

The house was acquired by Stephen Phillips in the early 1900s. His great-grandfather, Captain Stephen Phillips, built a house at 17 Chestnut Street in 1804, soon after the street was laid out. The family has long been active in Salem and national public service.

When Stephen Phillips died in 1971, he left this house in trust to be open to the public. It was his wish that the original furnishings would remain. The furnishings include examples of early American, English, and Dutch pieces as well as items from the Far East and Polynesia gathered over five generations by the Phillipses, and the Duncans, Pingrees, and the Wheatlands who married into the family.

The china collection is outstanding, embracing as it does a very wide variety of Chinese export porcelain as well as French and English. The oriental rugs are exceptional, with several extremely rare antique Persian and Chinese carpets. Also on display are unusually fine primitive wood carvings from the numerous South Pacific islands visited by the family's sailing ships. Colonial paintings, watercolors, and prints, together with choice bronzes, porcelains, lacquers, and jades grace this beautiful home of a wealthy sea captain and merchant from Salem's great seafaring days. In addition to the furnishings, the house is noted for McIntire's woodwork, especially the delicately carved mantles in the original front rooms.

The library, with a detail of McIntire's mantle carving.

Behind the arched doors of the brick carriage house are elegant carriages used by the family in the preceding century and two Pierce-Arrow cars used fifty years ago.

Open to the public Memorial Day weekend to mid-October. Closed Sundays. Admission charged. (Tel. 617-744-0440).

(above) Dining room is a Colonial Revival addition to the house, with Pingree family china on the table. (left) McIntire carving from sitting-room mantle.

(above) Numbers 38–40 Chestnut Street with the Phillips House at right. (below) Phillips Carriage House and newly restored brougham.

*One of Chestnut Street's most beautiful contemporary
treasures is the spring garden maintained by Helen Usher.*

(above) Afternoon light accents the details of the brick mansions along the South side of Chestnut Street. (left) Spring blossoms color the yard of the McIntire-designed Butman-Waters House (1806) on Cambridge Street, just off Chestnut.

Pickering Wharf, with its water-front restaurants, marina, and shops, welcomes residents and tourists alike. A popular attraction is "The Voyage of the India Star," a multimedia program that re-creates Salem as it was in the early nineteenth century.

(above left and right) Salem's old Town Hall (1827) has become the focal point of the many restored Federal period commercial buildings in Salem's downtown. The Town Hall has a gallery and the offices of the Chamber of Commerce. (left) First Church, built in 1835, at 316 Essex Street, is on the site of Salem's first meetinghouse.

House of the Seven Gables
54 Turner Street

America's most famous literary house, and perhaps the most visited historic dwelling in New England, is the House of the Seven Gables.

More properly called the Turner-Ingersoll House, the house was made famous by Nathaniel Hawthorne's novel and it was first opened to the public as part of a charitable institution.

Built in 1668 by Captain John Turner, the house was expanded several times by the Turners as the family prospered, eventually acquiring its seven gables and a lean-to. By 1782, however, hard times forced John Turner III to sell the house and it was acquired by Cap-

(above) "Phoebe's Room" in the Gables. (right) Gables Dining room. (opposite) The Gables with its beautiful spring garden, planted under the direction of Daniel Foley.

tain Samuel Ingersoll, whose wife, Susannah, was Hawthorne's cousin. The Ingersoll's daughter, Susannah, was a local historian and she was often visited by Hawthorne. Her stories and the house itself became the basis for his famous novel.

The house, then somewhat altered with some of the gables removed, passed out of the Ingersoll family in 1889 and was finally acquired by Caroline O. Emmer-

ton. She had established a settlement house and she restored the House of the Seven Gables as an attraction to provide a source of funds to support the charitable work.

(opposite) Nathaniel Hawthorne birthplace.   *(above) Kitchen in the Hawthorne birthplace.*

Miss Emmerton's project is a success story. The settlement house, situated just a block away on Derby Street, continues to be an important civic institution in Salem, and the Gables restoration project has grown into a complex of five restored historic and architecturally significant buildings.

The Gables was opened to the public in 1910. The following year Miss Emmerton purchased the Hooper-Hathaway House (1686) and moved it to the site. The Retire Beckett House (1655) was acquired in 1916 and moved to its present location in 1926. It now serves as the gift shop except during the winter months. Hawthorne's birthplace was moved to the site in 1958. Built about 1750, this house was bought by Captain Daniel Hawthorne in 1772, and his grandson, Nathaniel, was born here in 1804. The Counting House (c.1840), built next to the Gables, was moved to its present location beside Salem harbor.

The Gables is open all year; the other buildings surrounding the magnificent garden are open in the summer only. Admission charged. (Tel. 617-744-0991)

Salem Common

This area was set aside as a training field in 1714 but it was so swampy that the land was used mostly for grazing cattle. During the prosperous days at the turn of the eighteenth century a public subscription sponsored by Elias Hasket Derby, 2nd, raised funds to fill and level the ground, make walls, plant Lombardy poplars, and erect a fence. Samuel McIntire was hired to create gates for the entrances. In 1802 the common and the streets around it were renamed Washington Square.

The beautification of the area made it an attractive neighborhood, and soon the wealthy began constructing homes that rivaled those on Chestnut Street. The large brick mansions along Washington Square North were built between 1818 and 1830. On Washington Square East is a fine Greek Revival house and another large house built in the Colonial Revival style (left). McIntire's arches were removed in 1850, but a reproduction (right) one-quarter size of the original was constructed in 1976.

(*above*) *Brick mansions along Washington Square North.*
(*left*) *Number 39–41 Washington Square North was built in 1830, at the end of the Federal period, and it has several Greek Revival elements.*

The Eleazer Gedney House, at 21 High Street, was built in 1665 and has been altered several times over the years. The house passed out of the Gedney family in 1773 and it was used by tenants until 1962 when the interior was stripped to reveal the architectural details. Acquired in 1967 by the Society for the Preservation of New England Antiquities, the house is used to show students construction details usually hidden by finish work. At left is the caretaker's house, which dates from the late eighteenth century. The Gedney House is not regularly open to the public. For more information contact the SPNEA, 141 Cambridge Street, Boston, Massachusetts 02114 (tel. 617-227-3956).

Witch House
310½ Essex Street

According to tradition, preliminary examinations for the 1692 witch trial were held in this house. Jonathan Corwin, owner of the house, and another magistrate, John Hathorne, presided over the hearings.

The two men, along with everyone else, were swept up in the witch-hunt fervor. The stories told by the so-called bewitched girls resulted in the execution of twenty people and imprisonment of some 150 others before reason finally prevailed.

Built about 1642, the Witch House was remodeled by Corwin in 1674–75 and was further altered several times before it was acquired and restored by the city in the mid-1940s. Now managed by the Salem Parks Department, the house has many fine seventeenth-century furnishings.

Open March through November. Admission charged. (Tel. 617-744-0180)

(above) Many school groups visit the Witch House annually, especially toward the end of October, when Halloween events are scheduled in the city. (opposite above) The dining room. (opposite below) Second-floor chamber is where the witch pretrial examinations were conducted.

57

Pioneer Village
Forest River Park

One of Salem's lesser-known attractions, and one that lends itself nicely to visits by children, is this reproduction of Salem in 1630. Constructed in 1930 as the city's contribution to the Massachusetts Bay tercentenary, the village is a collection of authentically built houses and other dwellings of the period. The two-story governor's house, two thatch-roofed cottages, sod-roofed dugouts, and a bark-covered wigwam make up the village. Pillory and stocks, gardens, and other outdoor exhibits are on display. The houses are sparsely furnished and children can enjoy the site without close supervision — something not permitted in most of the other attractions in the city.

To find the village, follow Lafayette Street (Rte. 114) east toward Marblehead and turn left on West Street at the traffic lights by Salem State College. The village is part of Forest River Park, which also offers swimming and picnic tables.

Operated by the Salem Parks Department, Pioneer Village is open June through October. Admission charged. (Tel. 617-744-0180)

The Peabody Museum of Salem
East India Square, 161 Essex Street

During the eighteenth and nineteenth centuries, marine societies were formed in many seaports to assist widows and children of deceased members and to gather and share information regarding navigation. Salem's East India Society began like the others but, to the lasting credit of its members, its 1799 charter included a provision for creating a museum.

In the early 1800s, Salem's merchant fleet reached ports throughout the world. The objects brought home by the sea captains who were members of the society form the basis of the collections at the Peabody Museum. East India Marine Hall (above), now a National Historic Landmark, was built in 1824 to house the growing collection and as a meeting place for the society. Other additions were made over the years, with the most recent major expansion completed in 1976.

The Peabody Museum's collections represent three major areas: the maritime history of New England, the

life-styles of non-European peoples, and the natural history of New England. They include: ship models, marine paintings, portraits and prints, figureheads, sailors' artifacts, scrimshaw, historical fishing implements, and navigational instruments. The collections also feature textiles, carvings, pottery, jewelry, weapons, musical instruments, household items, and religious artifacts from Japan, China, Korea, Southeast Asia, India and the Himalayas; China Trade material, including porcelain, paintings, furniture, and other decorative wares; and Pacific Island material, including carvings, clothing, weapons, tools and utensils. The natural history exhibits include a comprehensive collection of New England plants, birds, mammals, fish, reptiles, amphibians, and seashore life.

A library of nearly one-hundred thousand volumes, plus log books, maps and charts, and a photographic collection of over one million prints and negatives relating to the museum's collections is open to the public for research. The museum shop offers a wide and varied selection of books, reproductions,

(above) Figureheads in East India Marine Hall are among the Peabody's most colorful exhibits. (right) Masks from the Bismark Archipelago are part of the Polynesian collection. Salem ships brought the first Westerners to many of the Pacific islands.

(above) East India Hall, the oldest section of the museum, includes many paintings, figureheads, and larger exhibits. (right) Outrigger canoe is a two-thirds scale model made in the Western Caroline islands in 1966. At left is a rare statue of Hawaiian War God, Kukailimoku, one of only three such carvings in existence. When missionaries reached these islands, most of the wooden "idols" were destroyed.

marine prints, unusual gift items, post cards, jewelry, and folk toys. Programs, courses, and other special events are offered throughout the year by the museum's education department.

As the oldest continuously operating museum in

the country, the Peabody Museum is open daily throughout the year, except Thanksgiving, Christmas, and New Year's Day. The library and offices are open weekdays only. Admission charged. For general information call 617-745-1876; for exhibits information, call 617-745-9500.

Another figurehead fills a window in the new wing of the museum. (below) Students learn about Grand Banks fishing dories while on a museum tour. Groups are welcome at most of Salem's attractions but advance reservations are usually required. Guided tours for individuals are also available at the Peabody Museum.

MAUDE G AMERO

Interior of the Bonded Warehouse.

Salem Maritime
National Historic Site
Derby Street

The wealth that made possible the grand Federal period mansions that attract visitors to Salem today came from the sea. Salem maintained an active merchant fleet from the late seventeenth century, but it was from the end of the Revolutionary War until about 1820 that Salem reached its pinnacle of importance as a seaport. During these years Elias Hasket Derby became America's first millionaire, and the wharf that bears his family name was always lined with vessels unloading exotic goods or being loaded with trade cargoes for ports throughout the world.

Today's Maritime National Historic Site was the center for seaport activity. Operated by the National Park Service since 1937, the nine-acre site is open to the public all year without charge.

The centerpiece for the site is the Custom House, built in 1819 just before the seaport began to decline. Nathaniel Hawthorne worked here in the late 1840s and his desk is on display. Next door is the Hawkes House, designed by Samuel McIntire and used by Derby during the Revolution as a warehouse for prize

cargoes captured by his fleet of privateers. Behind the Custom House is the Bonded Warehouse, where goods were stored awaiting re-export or payment of import duties.

The Derby House, built in 1761–62 for Elias Derby, is Salem's oldest brick dwelling. Next to it is the West India Goods Store, built in the early 1800s and now open to the public as a coffee house. Behind the main buildings are the scale house with its weighing equipment, and the Narbonne House, built before 1671, and not open to the public.

Across Derby Street is Derby wharf, begun about 1762, Salem's longest and busiest wharf for many years. At one time there were fourteen warehouses on this wharf and one hundred in the city. The lighthouse at the end of the half-mile-long wharf was erected as a range light in 1871.

The Salem Maritime National Historic Site is open daily all year. (Tel. 617-744-4323)

(opposite) The brig **Leander** was built in 1821 and sailed in the China and Mediterranean trade until the 1840s. This model in the Bonded Warehouse was made in 1926 for the city's 300th anniversary.

The Custom House has offices restored to the period. Visitors may watch a film presentation on Salem's maritime history. The Hawks House, center, is not open to the public but the Derby House, right, with rooms restored and furnished to about the time of the Revolution, is open on scheduled tours.

Elias Derby's house is the oldest brick dwelling in the city.

The Narbonne House, built before 1671, is part of the site and also fronts on Essex Street.

A Brief History of Marblehead

Many coastal communities have lost their ties with the sea, but not Marblehead. Founded as a fishing station in 1629, Marblehead has as strong a seagoing tradition today as it did when its fleets sailed the Grand Banks in search of cod. Of course, today's fleet is mostly pleasure sailboats but the feeling that locals and visitors alike have for the sea is evident throughout the community.

For its first twenty years Marblehead was under the jurisdiction of Salem, but the stern, religious Puritans were in constant conflict with the freethinking, unruly fishermen of Marblehead. In 1648 Marblehead was granted independence from Salem.

Situated on a rocky, hilly peninsula, Marblehead could never have developed as a farming community. Instead, from its first settlement until the mid-nineteenth century, Marblehead made its living from the sea. As early as 1660 the town was considered the fishing capital of New England. From local waters to the Grand Banks, the fishermen returned with their catch and cured the fish for export to Europe and the West Indies.

Eventually Marblehead's sailors turned to foreign trade as well as fishing, and by the time of the Revolutionary War, prosperous Marblehead was the second-largest town in Massachusetts. Wealthy merchants and

View of Marblehead Harbor and Marblehead Neck from the tower of Abbot Hall. Marblehead Neck is mostly residential, although a large area is reserved for an Audubon sanctuary. There are several yacht clubs, and at the far end are a small park and Marblehead Light, a beacon for mariners.

captains built many of the homes that still line the streets of the old town.

Marblehead was generous with financial support, ships and men during the Revolutionary War. Who can forget that crews of Marblehead sailors manned the boats that ferried Washington across the Delaware? But few people are aware that the end of the war left Marblehead with some four hundred widows and hundreds more fatherless children. While many other New England seaports, most notably nearby Salem, boomed in the years between the wars with the British, Marblehead suffered economically because it had given so generously of its men and money in the Revolution. Salem today is colored by the quality and quantity of its Federal period architecture, but Marblehead retains its colonial, or Georgian, image because few men were wealthy enough to build in the grand Federal style after the Revolution.

Difficulties before and during the War of 1812 further dampened Marblehead's economy, although the town again sent men and ships to fight the British. After this war, Marblehead ships and seamen were active in the gold rush and the China Trade. Trade and prosperity returned for a while, although the community and its fishing fleet received another blow when the great storm of 1846 destroyed ships and took the lives of sixty-five men.

During the latter half of the nineteenth century, activity in small New England seaports declined, and Marblehead, like most of the others, turned to manufacturing. Shoemaking, already an important winter home industry by the early 1800s, expanded when factories were built about mid-century in the newer section of town that developed away from the waterfront. In 1831 the railroad reached the community, and by

A view along Franklin Street in the old town. Houses are built close to the street; in some places there is no room for sidewalks.

Marblehead's unusual powder house, located on Green Street, was built in 1755 in what was then a rural location.

1837 the value of manufactured goods was more than double the value of fisheries. The prosperity was short lived, however, for fires in 1877 and 1888 destroyed the factories and other businesses.

Fortunately, the fires spared the old town. Unlike Portsmouth and Newburyport, where fires gutted the centers of the towns and destroyed hundreds of Colonial structures, Marblehead's old town has survived nearly intact from the end of the eighteenth century.

Marblehead's role in the Revolution was celebrated in 1876, highlighted by the laying of the cornerstone for Abbot Hall on July 4 in that year. The hall, which is open daily, houses the town offices and many historical artifacts and paintings. The most famous item is *The Spirit of '76*, painted by Archibald Willard and given to the town by native son General John H. Devereux to honor the brave men of Marblehead.

By the end of the nineteenth century Marblehead had again turned to the sea, developing into a popular summer resort. Although the first settlers built their homes near Little Harbor where their boats were moored, larger Marblehead Harbor became the center of resort activity. Today some two thousand pleasure yachts, most of them sailboats, and six yacht clubs give credence to Marblehead's claim that it is the "Yachting Capital of America."

No longer a center of fishing or manufacturing, Marblehead today is a residential community that nevertheless retains its ties to the past. The importance of Marblehead's collection of architectural treasures was recognized in 1968 when the major portion of the old town was declared a historic district. Few other American communities have retained their colonial charm without needing massive restoration. Marblehead's buildings have been retained, spared from fires and from the rebuilding that comes from economic booms. Today we treasure the winding, narrow streets and the old houses that cling to the rocky shore and hillsides.

Jeremiah Lee Mansion
161 Washington Street

Although Marblehead has a wealth of architecturally significant buildings, only a handful are open to the public. Fortunately, one of the latter is perhaps the most impressive house ever built in Marblehead — the Lee Mansion.

Jeremiah Lee was a wealthy merchant in the years before the Revolution. His fleet carried on a lively trade between America, Europe, and the West Indies. An ardent patriot, he was a member of the Committee of Safety and might well have become a leader in the war effort had he not died in 1775.

Lee built his mansion in 1768. Designed in the great Georgian style of a London town house, the mansion has long been considered one of the finest of its type in the country. Rich carving and paneling accent the large rooms, which have been furnished to reflect Lee's era. The paneling, staircase, and wallpaper are original.

Lee's widow, Martha, lived in the house after his death. Eventually it was acquired by Chief Justice Samuel Sewall, then became a bank for more than a century until it was taken over in 1909 by the Marblehead Historical Society. In years past, the mansion has housed such guests as Washington, Lafayette, Monroe, and Jackson.

The Lee Mansion is open daily, except Sunday, from mid-May through mid-October. Admission charged. (Tel. 617-631-1069)

The facade of the Lee Mansion is built of wood in a style that resembles stone.

(above) The Lee Mansion state dining room where banquets and receptions were held. (right) A guest bedroom.

(below) The Lee Mansion dining room. Bouquets were especially made for a summer reception. Around the fireplace are rare Sadler and Green tiles dating from the early eighteenth century. (right) The drawing room.

(above) Colonial home owners often painted their houses in bright colors. On Lee Street, today's residents continue the tradition. (left) St. Michael's Church, Summer Street, built in 1714, is one of the oldest Episcopal churches in America. Open to the public weekdays 9 a.m. to 3 p.m.(tel. 617-631-0657). (opposite above) View along High Street with the steeple of Old North Church in the background. Built in 1825, the church is open to the public by contacting the church office, 10 Stacey Street, (tel. 631-1244). (opposite below) The Lafayette House, at the corner of Lee and Union streets, is so named because tradition has it that when Lafayette visited Marblehead, a portion of this house had to be removed to allow passage of Lafayette's carriage.

Burial Hill is one of the highest points in Marblehead. Many of the town's earliest settlers and most famous people are buried here along with some six hundred men who died during the Revolution. The stones, some dating to the 1600s, reflect the varied designs of the stonecutter's art.

Little Harbor, photographed from Gerry Island. It was here that the first settlers of Marblehead erected their homes and fish drying stages. The small islands provided shelter for the small fishing boats, and nearby Burial Hill was a good place for a lookout and for the first meetinghouse.

King Hooper Mansion
8 Hooper Street

Built in two stages, the first in 1728, and the front Georgian section in 1747, this building was the home of Robert Hooper, a wealthy merchant whose living style earned him the sobriquet of "king." Hooper was a Tory during the Revolution and had to leave town, although he returned after the war.

In 1938, the house was purchased and restored to become the home of the Marblehead Arts Association. Several period rooms are open to the public (admission charged), and the third-floor ballroom is now the art gallery with monthly exhibits (no charge). The house is open daily in the afternoons, except January and February. (Tel. 617-631-2608)

(above) Marblehead Harbor. (left) Closely placed houses rising up to Abbot Hall give the town a European village appearance. (below) Sailboat races viewed from Fort Sewall.

Marblehead's old town house was built in 1727 at what is now called Market Square. For 150 years, until the construction of Abbot Hall, this was the center of local government.